Rabbit Tracks

Rabbit Tracks

The Poetry of Nature

poems by

Joseph Carosella

SHANTI ARTS PUBLISHING

BRUNSWICK, MAINE

Rabbit Tracks The Poetry of Nature

Copyright 2025 Joseph Carosella

Published by Shanti Arts LLC

Designed by Shanti Arts Designs

193 Hillside Road
Brunswick, Maine 04011
shantiarts.com

Cover image David Castor, Rabbit Tracks in the Snow, 2013.
Wikimedia Commons. Public Domain.

Interior images 10 11 annie-spratt P57i4zlYjQg unsplash.com 42
43 gary-walker-jones PYun-IgNAnE unsplash.com 72 73 johannes-
plenio EOIToTneyZ4 unsplash.com 104 105 joel-jasmin-forestbird
efuwb5eBDrI unsplash.com.

Printed in the United States of America

ISBN 978-1-962082-90-7 softcover

LCCN 2026931304

To my parents, Joseph V. and Laura E.
they gave me the intertwined gifts of nature and poetry.

To Diury
who, along with love has brought balance and moderation,
which is no easy task,
since she lives with an Enneagram Seven .

To Emilia, Mattias, and Vitas
they have brought *Whole Child, Whole Parent* to life.

To my Team of Light
they never stop tag-teaming as guides and muses.

And of course, to my Anam Cara
who has always been there, even if I didn't know it.

Whole Child, Whole Parent, by Polly Berrien-Berends

The author wishes to thank Christine Cote of Shanti Arts
for her encouragement and flexibility,
and for bringing *Rabbit Tracks* to life.

Contents

Fall

Spring's Delights

To sit outside, this second day of spring,
to sit and listen as the songbirds sing
those who've returned and those who braved the snow
in morning cold, well-pleased that soon a mellow
breath and nearer sun will warm the days
and bright and cheery blooms bring their displays
of blue or pink or yellow even white,
which lately spoke of snow the growing light
unfolds the fulsome heart as winter fades,
unclasps its chilly grip, and spring's parades
return to us return us to a vernal ease
thank God, I say, for such delights as these.

Kibby Pond in March

March 23

The oscillating nights and days
of March are fine for sugaring
the sun-warmed sap upsurges to
the taps to turn itself into
a sweet elixir.
Northern walks through snowy woods
in March are less divine.
The snow projects the pre-dawn chill
but don't be fooled.
With every second step you sink
below the crust
and often dip your boot into a rill
the snowshoes stayed behind .
But worse is never knowing
when you'll sink.
Each time surprises, startling, tipping.
Squiggling tracks
show your control of stride subsides,
despite your hope,
to plonking awkward tipsy steps.
But when you reach the pond
and rest on rocks
and soak in silence, solitude and sun,
ah, well,
the trudge you took through
softened snow recedes,
and grace returns.

Waking with Windows Open

April 8

So eager that they can't wait for the dawn
they start their songs in dark and burst their breasts
their fervent mating ardor lifts and crests
I'm here, they call. *I claim this patch with song,
and if you're willing, I'll claim you, and our
duet shall state that here, with tufts and sticks,
we pledge to build both avian hope and bower,
and brood and feed and fledge our coming chicks.*
Committed to the core of every hollow
bone and spring-fresh feather, forth they trill,
proclaiming this year's plan. I wake and follow
through the open windows, rapt, and thrilled,
the sounds of early April life fulfilled.

In Erebus Country

April 10

We walk, just two of us, up mountains. Up,
then down through open leafless April woods.
The burly sun has brushed off every cloud,
thus nearly every nook and forest fold
is reached and warmed by his irradiant strength.
Two thrumming grouse wing up when we approach,
two vernal ponds redound with calls of eager
lovesick croakers seeking mating trysts.
A lonely raven glides above the ridge,
on endless circling quest. Boot strides upon
the crumbling leafy mold and needles set
off woodsy scents, combined with sweet caressing
breezes nose and lungs and skin join in
the joy of treading feet and feasting ears
and eyes. And mind is filled as heart is filled
and soothed with Adirondack hiking grace.

Apricot Tree

April 12

Our apricot, which never bore
because its mate died years before
it came to its maturity,
is covered now, for all to see,
in luscious, fragrant blooms.
As if it knew its time has come
such barren years can anyone
have been more patient than was I?
Yet now it seems to ask me why
I feel I can presume.
To take a life, pragmatically,
is commonplace. Am I not free
to use my saw? The apricot
must yield. Instead, a hazelnut
will grow. And yet for whom
in its last spring, does it bring forth
this blossoming, this bold rebirth.
I ask, as beauteous boughs uplift
is this admonishment, or gift?

April Snow

April 16

What the hell mid-April snow?
What's that supposed to mean, or show?
The gods above must like a laugh
is this to thresh the wheat from chaff?
But even winter fans like me
find snowfall now a travesty
of springtime's ever milder march
toward balm. Their sense of humor's arch.
OK, the snow won't last, and yet
we feel aggrieved. I'd like to bet
if the tables turned they would get surly,
like hungry bears awakened early.
Yet what can mortals undertake
against such snow besides to shake
our fists, and curse for April's sake.

Night Currents

April 24

Slipping into easy Sleep at ten
I wake at one and wonder why.
I toss and turn and toss again,
no luck, alas. Maybe a lullaby
would nudge me back to Nod, but Silence reigns,
too late for love, too soon for fowl.
I lie, adrift, in Dark's domain,
alone, no comfort even from an owl.

Right There, In the Forsythia

Their bush is next to where I park my car.
They perch and flit and call and sing. To us?
Sometimes it seems that way, that they are friends.
Mostly they aren't afraid of us,
unless we notice them too fixedly.
I speak to both of them, though one seems more
my type than does the other.
Creamy white and tan, they're beautiful.
They must have names but I am ignorant of that.
I do know, though, that I admire
how they live their lives.
Straightforward and with diligence
they do what they must do.
They have no time to write a poem.
But listen to them sing!

Blue, Yellow, Green

April 30

Oh, what a joy to stare at this blue sky
through clumps of maple seeds that soon will fly
pale yellow, with a hint of green they wait
till time and wind release them to their fate.
They'll maybe sprout just where they land, and then
I'll weed them out. Next year they'll try again.
For now, though, there they hang against the blue,
a simple, pretty, end-of-April view.

Cake or Ice Cream?

I looked up, wondering what I'd see.
Cape Breton Island, or the Isle of Skye?
On clouds all traveling is free.
It's easy. Though to soar you must rely
on nimble thoughts and letting go.
The Earth is gorgeous listen, hear the birds?
Showers, flowers, breezes oh,
the Spring! And other pleasures using words,
eating, hiking, loving, books.
Down here I find so much to revel in.
The beauty's there if I just look.
But seeing clouds and stars, I look within
and up they call as they glide by.
This life of ours is good. But, ah, the Sky.

Ferns

May 5

It's early May, a little after one.
The trees with leaf are still not fully clothed.
The fiddleheads stand friendly in the sun.
They wave to me and one another, bold.
Last week they weren't here I would've seen
They stand there now, like Robin's Men in green,
his Merrie Men, attentive should he call,
Each one himself, yet dutiful to all.
In bright pale fronds they form a troop
yet seem more individuals than group.
And soon they'll spend their days in deeper shade,
their hue more somber, as in shadowed glade,
and reaching out, they'll touch, not one will stray
and loyal to the company they'll stay.
How is it that I've never seen this stage
of ferny independence in mid-Spring?
Is this their yearly way to come of age?
I'm sorry that till now I've missed this thing.

Locust and Maple

May 7

By chance I craned my neck from there
beneath the bright-blue, chilly morning
smile of God, to see the Locust
and the Maple in my yard.
Maple in sea-green leafy dress
with whirligigs for seeding.
Locust stark, its limbs and twigs
asleep still, or just lazy.
Maple has sent her children down
to root in lawn and garden bed.
Locust seems to have no thought
of spring. He will not rush.
Or needs more time. And maybe that
is why God smiles, to see these two,
together now for more years than
I've lived, still marking seasons both
in their own ways. And if God's mirth
extends to them, well, mightn't God
bestow a bit on us as well?
For we must also find our way
at our own pace, each year, each day.
And whether I'm more like Maple or
like Locust, I should keep in mind
that other rhythms besides mine
are more than welcome in God's world.

Queen May

May 10

Alyssum white, lobelia blue
gentle, vibrant, fragrant, true.
Humble sedum, on the ground,
marigold orange for your crown.
And piquant mint for merry spice.
O, queenly May, your gifts entice
us to rejoice in springtime bliss.
What better birthday month than this?

O Pemptos Anemos

May 16

The eastern wind announces birth
and hails all new beginnings.
It's light and joyous springtime air,
a-bloom with promise, and we waft
on Euros into this new world.

The southern summer wind is full
of heavy verdant growth, and drive.
We make not only hay on days
of sun, but plans, pulled by ambition
and the inner urge of life,
and Notos' passion-heated breath.

In fall the western wind of Zephyr
brings the harvest gratitude
of things well done, and of their fruits.
But hanging on its edge a warning
blows, of change, a downward turn,
of energies now spent. And oh,
the melancholy bittersweet
awareness of the creep of time.

At last the cycle turns and we
face north the fierce and bitter Boreas
sweeps down to scour, blast and force
us to ring in the season of
remaking and renewal. All
around is death and dormancy
and like the trees, we must accept

that we must die a little, giving
up what once we were, so that
we overhaul ourselves both in
and out and store some strength for our
next step, whichever way it leads.

And thus both winds and seasons mark
the timeless passages of time.
But what of the unrecognized
fifth wind? The Greeks left it unnamed.
I feel its power nonetheless.
It isn't tied in one direction,
and it can blow across the years,
and differently for you and me,
perhaps. This is the wind that calls
us to become what we can be.
The wind of transformation, coaxing,
prodding us, reminding standing
still can't be how best we live.
Snakes shed their skin and tadpoles morph.
And butterflies were recently less lovely
now they dance upon the breeze,
the fifth and final wind.

Morning Glory May

May 17

The sky is early blue,
the sun dips gold
upon the locust tops.
Although it's cold
I sit
and watch, with tea,
the day unfold.
Small birds seem big they sing
so brave and bold.
And other miracles behold
the lilies of the valley,
squirrels that scold,
the grace of ferns, the cooing
doves all told
it is a morning glory,
one to hold
inside the heart, where
beauty can't grow old.

Jenny

May 18

Creeping Jenny, yellow-green
with glowing lustrous, lovely sheen.
She gives the forward deck-edge grace,
gladly filling in that space.
This year I note her growing higher,
a ground-cover somehow inspired
to go beyond, to maximize
her growth, above official size.
If plants do yoga, this is Tree
reaching for the sky to see
what self-improvement can come from
ambition and a little sun.
I keep my Jenny company
I can't resist, I want to see
what she achieves. And whether I
can match her drive, and touch the sky.

Glad I Got Up

May 21

There's something soft about the
pre-dawn light of May.
Locust trees will soon leaf out
though all their cousins have gone green,
and glow in the slowly, gently starting day.
The moon's past full, and lazy, peeks
around grim clouds,
half-winking, proud.
Letting me know that for these weeks
her job is done.
But lilac, honeysuckle and their friends
are still at work, and so perfume the air
with sweetest scents
before the sun
lights up the very early hour.
But I don't wish myself in bed
I'll take, instead,
the eagerness of the flowers.
Tonight I may look back and say
this was, by far,
the best part of today.

Lesson from a Chipmunk

May 24

I set some millet out to feed my friends
the sparrows, salted sunflower seeds as well.
Who came for breakfast was a chipmunk, though.
She started at one end of what I'd strewn
and munched methodically each morsel, grazing
gladly. Did she wonder as she filled her
cheeks how that abundance came to lie
in her small patch of life. She looked at me
now and again, but did she know the hand
that gave her all that she could eat? And when
the startling seeds of plenty come my way
will I devour them without a thought
or see the hand of generosity
and look at God a time or two, in thanks.

Woodchuck

May 25

Four times the woodchuck ventured out
then hesitated, with her snout
inspecting, sniffing at the air
and noting I was sitting there
beside the deck. Four times she ducked
back down below. Then courage stuck
and off she ran across the yard
to feed somewhere, still on her guard.
How different is her life from mine
a fisher, finding her, would dine,
or else a fox. I face no threats,
my bills are paid, my table set,
and I can sit and dream and write,
while life for her is fear and flight.

What Do I Know?

This morning's sky has clouds of texture
like ginkgo leaves, laid out like fans.
I'm not sure why, but I conjecture
that when God stops and earthward scans
such cloud-play may bring on a smile.
Then God may rest from labors great
and simply marvel for a while
at all that's wondrous. Though the state
of human struggle still we hate
wage war, discriminate, revile
must daily cause God pain and grief.
Perhaps in moments of repose
and admiration, God's belief
in our potential lives, or grows.
If I were God, sometimes I'd doubt
that we will ever sort things out.
Yet watching clouds, I might suppose
I'm ignorant, and trust God knows.

Locust Eater

You know the honey locust tree
dark-barked, it towers regally
above the maples, leafing late
and dropping pods to propagate,
as well as spiny twigs beware.
And yet I love these locusts fair
of form, and fairer yet of blooms,
which scent bright May with sweet perfume.
These blossoms fall in soft cascade,
an intermittent white parade
adorning all beneath their boughs.
But here is something no one knows
they taste as sweet as they do smell
in double strings, like silent bells,
they hang. I pluck and strip their stems
and in they go, these diadems.
I savor them and thank the trees
for all their gifts, including these.

Patio Plants

May 30

Both blue lobelia and some purple ones
we have in pots out back are keeping company
with parsley, dill, arugula, with basil,
other flowers. Also chamomile.
We've never had ten pots before. Why not,
though. They look happy. When I look at them
I'm happy, too. But living in a little
pot means they can only grow so much.
Is that enough for them? Are they content
to live within the limits I've set out?
Somehow I feel that I should offer
more. For plants as well as people where's
the line between contentment and a longing
to reach out and go beyond. It's said
that those who do not want have all they need.
That is a trick that I would like to learn.
Back to the potted plants they seem to feel
the moment is the key. They exude joy
and beauty and a daily grace. Perhaps
a little will rub off on me. Perhaps
with help from them, I'll figure all this out.

Clearing Skies, and Heart

May 31

Three or four days of rain
who can remember . . . ?
then the sky blues.
I don't know what it's like in the city,
but in our village, the park, the lake, our yard
all shine fresh and rinsed.
I walk, then plant tomatoes.
Eat some supper, mow.
And just like that,
I am renewed.

Revelation

June 7

The birds got up, then so did I
to hark to them and search the sky.
Their songs' import I could not learn.
But looking, saw within the turn
of Earth a message meant for me?
How near to us Eternity.

Little Teacher

June 7

The inch-worm isn't quite an inch.
It drifts about on silken thread.
It doesn't fear the wind, or flinch.
By gentle morning airs it's led
to light somewhere and meet its fate.
Nor it, nor I can tell that yet.
How long before it changes state
I've no idea. I watch it let
life happen to it as it may.
I wonder, should I follow suit
and leave off planning for each day,
content that every one bears fruit?

Faeries

June 11

The ones I seek are not those people dread
they don't leave changelings in a newborn's bed,
nor spoil the milk, nor give your heart a tweak
so you change love for jealousy. They wreak
no havoc here. We cause our woes ourselves,
or they are sent to us. These faerie elves
live near and maybe wonder why we miss
what makes their eyes shine bright the simple bliss
of meadows, sylvan webs, the pond frog's croak,
the stars at night, the majesty of oak.
The pink of dawn, and bird tracks in the snow,
the scent of spruce and mint. Could God bestow
upon us more than this? If we could see
with faerie hearts the kindly harmony
surrounding us, why we, too, might grow wings
and flit, and smile at such lovely things.

Bee Bold

June 13

The bee is bold not bashful,
when it sweet nectar seeks
and shall we then be careful
and hold ourselves too meek
to drink when love Divine
contrives to slake our thirst?
The flowing cup a sign,
a gift. How well-rehearsed
in gratitude we ought
to be for gifts like these
how good the gracious thought
it's us God works to please.

Finding Your Way

June 18

Woods and woods, and yet more woods
eight hours, sixteen miles.
Trails some muddy, others good
a climb, then bushwhack trials
underbrush and horseflies, sweat,
and map and compass error.
Struggles that ultimately let
the trail shine all the fairer.
When once again we'd found the Way
our step was light. No strain
to tread the track that others lay
but then, where is the gain?

Great Start!

June 21

A gray fox kit loped by and looked
then scrambled up a tree.
But right back down again it climbed,
investigating me.
You'd better go, I said. It paused,
then off it went once more.
I turned the corner, on the wall
a sibling stood. Both wore
black socks, and flicked their white-tipped tails.
We lingered as the early sun
eyed us, eyeing each other.
They flicked their heads. *We're done,*
they said, and lightly skipped away.
I stood in wonderment, well-pleased
and praised the generous day.

Chipmunk Holes

June 22

No sooner do I stop a hole,
the chipmunks dig another.
So little, but so brazen-bold
I wonder why I bother.
Some days I feel enough's enough
I ought to just play rough.
But every creature does its thing,
so how can I insist
that Nature just for me must sing?
Instead, we'll coexist.

Summer Is Here Again

June 24

The solstice came four days ago
the days must shorten now.
The joy that Summer's months bestow
is shadowed. Fall, somehow,
though months away, seems all too near.
But what is wrong with me?
The seasons pirouette each year,
and turn predictably.
So why lament at summer's start
when light and warmth abound?
Summer surely won't depart
before her time. Her crown
of verdant fullness sits just fine,
and our esteem's condign.
We'll live the summer day by day
let Autumn wait in line.

Heaven's Prism

Recently it came to me
our Sun must one day die.
Then all our Earth's great family
will perish. You and I,
of course, will go some years before.
We'll miss the cataclysm
that Heaven has in store.
Perhaps, though, Heaven's prism
will clarify our view
and maybe we will grasp God's plan
that Death and Life, those two
old friends, must hold each other's hand.

Rain

June 27

Rain outside I walked, got wet,
now by the window sit,
comfortable and dry. And yet
glad I went out in it.
Glad God's droplets came to pet
my body and my brain,
glad the two of us have met,
glad of nourishing rain.

Air Traffic Control

Can bees foretell the weather?
Where do they wait in rain?
From marigold or heather
today they must abstain.
And can they watch as patiently
as I, till raining stops
or fret to make their honey
and dance between the drops?
Indolent, I can regard
the placid, soothing scene
soft the raindrops rinse the yard
and leave a glistening sheen.
But for the bees it's all delay,
a morning whiled, gone.
I wonder if they, shivering, pray,
O, let the rain be done.

Black Cat

June 30

A black cat comes now visiting,
a-hunting in our yard.
A stealthy, sleek and graceful thing
the chipmunks are on guard.
Where she lives, what draws her by,
by what name she is known
all that remains a mystery.
Perhaps she lives alone.
Perhaps our street is now the site
where she must somehow thrive.
To prey on chipmunks is her right
if she is to survive.
I wish I knew her character,
I wish I knew her name.
I wish I didn't care for her.
To her, it's all the same.

June

June 30

Oh, June, my dear, must you then leave,
and give way to July?
It is ordained, and yet I grieve
to see your last silk sky.
To see the last dark mulberry
drop down to stain the ground,
to know your lithe Solstice fairy
will now be elsewhere bound,
to miss the evenings lingering long,
the gentlest, softest nights,
the earliest birds in joyous song,
the sweetest scents and sights . . .
Presiding over Spring's farewell
a privilege or a bane?
The passing days and weeks foretell
that never a month may deign
to slow Time's unrelenting flow
as even fools should know.
I am a fool. For me, dear June,
your last day comes too soon.

July

July 1

Welcome, Grande Olde Dame, July,
Queen of humid heat.
Sparking storms that lash the sky
to thunder's threatening beat.
Laying summer's heavy mantle
upon the woods and fields,
weighty, forceful, rarely gentle
Nature's might revealed.
Make the berries ripe and full.
Make the crops grow tall.
Forgo the toppling hail that culls,
the bolts that burn and brawl.
Mock us not with storms that punish,
grant us halcyon days.
Mark your footsteps light among us,
softening your ways.

Eating Jewels

July 1

Juice-stained lips and purple hands
mulberries abound
fruity amethysts I stand
and gobble all I've found.
In childhood sister, brother, I
we learned to eat these gems.
And still they shine, they rarify
a steamy morning in July,
these dripping diadems.

Bonus

July 16

Lavender, violet, purple, pink.
I went away. I didn't think
the mulberries would wait for me.
But yesterday I found a tree.
I plucked the ripe ones, chucked them in
my mouth. My lips, my hands, my skin
were dyed, a gorgeous, flashy proof
of plenty. When I'd had enough,
I said my thanks and went my way.
Guess what? I'm going back today!

July Heat

July 17

Sky candy, eye-candy, white shapes on blue,
cloud-shifting, clouds drifting aridly through.
Sun baking, sun taking sweat in great drops.
Hot July, hot and dry, baking the crops.
Deep glades with deep shade refuge to seek,
iced drinks, ah, nice drinks this hottest of weeks.
Eyes closing, eyes dozing ambition wanes
somnolence, indolence lethargy reigns.

Good Example

July 18

The rain falls tenderly and soft,
it blurs July's sharp edges
a mild missive from aloft,
from Heaven's angel judges,
reminding us with drops essential
that we must soften, too,
and see in everyone potential.
The rains come to renew
the shoots of hope faith reverential
and we? What shall we do?

Zucchini Flowers

July 22

Each year I plant a handful in some pots
and in a garden bed another few.
and then behold! some volunteers come up
in still more pots, and where the dahlias are.
That's how we have zucchini in the front
and on the side and in the back along
the deck. And every morning, rain or shine,
they show their optimism that the bees
will come to dust themselves in yellow pollen
meant to meet their drive for life, their urge
to procreate, by bringing forth their seeded
fruit. Sometimes I pick their smiling blooms,
dip them in egg and fry them for a treat.
Sometimes I let them be, to punctuate
the scene with merry color. Little suns,
they beam and radiate, proclaiming *Life!*
Ours may be brief, but in our day or two
we'll show you how to live. It isn't hard
give beauty, be of service and enjoy
the time you have. These humble, loyal, green
and golden plants are welcome every time.
You could do worse than have zucchini friends.

Berry Patch

July 30

Within the tall bushes
that hide you from others
you could be alone, yes,
just you and your pail. The
blue sky and blue berries.
But voices come forward.
Although disembodied,
you hear the words clearly.
It's like a church social
the talk is of cats and
of health, and Aunt Martha,
estate sales and travel
and butter on buns.
And blueberry muffins
and friends who annoy you.
You'd like them to take
a few breaths and be silent
and give you a bit
of a chance to reflect.
A patch of ripe berries
is nicer when quiet.
But thinking it over,
you have to be gracious.
Why shouldn't those voices
engage in their chat?
You came for the berries.
They came to be social.
There's room for you all
to be happy with that.

Serene

August 5

Early August, early morning . . .
a little locust leaf drifts down,
lands in my lap.
An underlit airliner bisects the blue,
flying south.
Wisps of cirrus waft up high,
bright from the east.
Birds call out their messages
over my head.
My pen writes my own message
summer.

Heat Waves

August 9

In heat waves, unlike bitter freezes,
days lose lustre anything that pleases
pleases less, and all things are diminished.
One waits for sweaty nights to finish,
gets up in listless ennui,
foggy of thought and sapped of energy,
yet still aware of dissipating meaning.
One wishes for an intervening
storm to rinse away malaise
and heat and enervating doldrum days,
to clear the air and mind of sluggishness
and make one light and bright, at last, and fresh.

Elderberry Times

August 11

A morning picking berries in the sun.
Glorious wild red and purple globes
of sour power tiny elderberries,
growing by the pond. My friends weren't home
and so I picked alone. Except I wasn't.
My mother taught us all about these gems
when we were kids, so she was there. Two sisters
and my brother, too, were company.
And then I heard some wings and looked a pair
of great blue herons, majesty in flight.
Some frogs lost patience on the bank and leapt
to splash the surface and attract the lazy
grazing out-sized carp. And I heard bees
and saw a wedge of geese, and felt the hum
of summer forest song. And even with
these goings-on and vivid memories
my berry morning by the pond brought peace.
I picked perhaps enough to fill three cups.
But actually, I came away with more.

Storm Play

August 11

When I was fourteen, full of foolish valor,
if summer storms approached and winds shook trees,
I'd climb the ashes out by our garage.
My father yelled *Come down from there!* His pallor
clear to me, I clamped my grip and knees
and clung the tighter in the storm's barrage.
To watch, protected on a porch on humid
August afternoons, a thunderstorm
sweep through, displaying overwhelming power,
is thrill enough. Yet sway with glee amid
the frightened leaves, on creaking limbs, and form
a deep exultant awe . . . That special hour
of storm-mad play
has marked me to this day.

It All Worked Out

August 12

I took out the bike and I went for a ride.
I wanted some ice cream some true bona-fide
and locally homemade that was my aim.
Cappie's it happened, was closed. Such a shame.
The bike jaunt was thus not the one that I'd planned.
But I rode past the river, deep woods and farmland,
saw two herons, a beaver, a woodchuck, a hawk
which is more than you get on the usual walk.
So I feasted on landscape instead of a cone.
And when I got back I had ice cream at home.

Making Friends

August 12

I stretch my hand out, you approach,
as jointly we agree to broach
this friendly possibility
though trust was missing previously,
we entertain a new rapport,
something we couldn't find before.
You see acceptance in my hand,
I'm trying more, to understand
your patterns and your point of view,
and meet you halfway. As for you,
you're not unwilling, just unclear
how to progress. I guess that's fear,
the product of experience.
And yet, you're giving me a chance.
We touch, still tentative.
It turns out to be nice
it's calmly lenitive.
The proofs suffice,
and so you lick me once or twice.

Bitter Freezes

Bitter freezes, unlike waves of heat,
spur you to action, they get you on your feet.
The air invigorates, each breath is rare
and pure, it cleanses, sharpens and prepares
you bold, decisive, eagerly you act.
Before the cold can chill your lower back,
or worse, befriend your toes, you are a flurry
of exertion, steaming breath and warming blood,
intent, engaged, oblivious to hurry,
for working in the cold, you know, does good.
Or if you're miles from home, out on a trail,
you think of mugs of tea or fireside ale,
and persevere until again toward
your hearth you stride, and that well-earned reward.
When winter, harsh and bitter, seizes
sleeping hills and trees in rime and squeezes
all, and grips it iron-clad, I'm glad.
I like deep freezes.

Stay a Little Longer, Please

August 15

After the August heatwave breaks
and sweaty days and sweaty nights
which had you dreaming of a lake
while scratching your mosquito bites
are past, the dawn is like September's.
Still weeks away, it calls remember!
Colder air and clearer sky
remind that summer, thus far a rock,
erodes before our anxious eye
just check the sunset by the clock . . .
Perhaps the seasons, equally
as melancholy as are we,
sharply feel what comes with fall
a fickle beauty, it presages
heavy hearts, decline, the call
of death, amid its crisp corsages.

August Calm

August 20

I can't yet see the sun itself
just how it lights the locust leaves.
They shine, as does the crescent moon.
A morning meant for soft reprieve.
The clouds of scallop-shell float by.
Metallic, glinting, airplanes arrow
straight on course across the sky.
Next month I'll be on one, today
I sit and sky-bathe, here I stay
to bask beneath the blue and white,
alive to August's acts and scenes
of gentle charm. Repose, not flight.
A morning to remain serene.

A Few Minutes Looking Up at Trees

Locust, pine, and maple, and some others,
stand and guard my yard, like elder brothers.
What chance is there for me to be as they,
stalwart, sage, accepting every day
as it may come, with grace, and maybe, even,
gratitude for life, a zest that leavens
day by day and year by year their slow
and faithful, uncomplaining stance. They show
me, if I look, through growth and dormancy
a trust, a patience and a constancy.
Will I be granted time enough, will I,
as they, earth-rooted, touch the sky?
Or still be chasing life until I die.

Come Again Sometime

August 28

I was sitting in the garage on a rainy day,
talking to Craig on the phone, you know,
catching up, and the rabbit,
who had been eyeing me a little,
from about eight feet away,
while eating grass under the wind chimes,
got spooked.
It came into the garage, then retreated,
came in, retreated, then came again, and,
I guess, wondered what I was doing there
and hopped right over to find out,
sniffing my sock-clad foot.
All this happened while I was talking.
We trusted each other to do no harm, and none was done.
After a bit, having scented me sufficiently,
it left and skittered out of sight
to do whatever was next on its rabbity list
for a wet afternoon.
That was my unusualest rabbit encounter ever,
being sniffed at by a little grass-flecked whiskered nose.
If it happened again, though, I wouldn't mind.

Playing Dead

August 30

This morning, early, on the road,
eyes open, but asleep for good
that's how and when I saw you. Possums'
lives aren't long not one-day blossoms,
but still, of short expectancy.
Coyotes, sure, can learn to see
that cars, unbending in their will
to rush ahead, can maim and kill.
But possums, simpler, steady, slow
how can we expect they'd know
the danger there. And is it fair?
It may be, many cars don't care.
One time, a possum lost, confused
climbed in our empty bin. Bemused,
it looked at me and I at it.
I'd never known one. I'll admit
that our eyes met. And how we see
comes from experience. Once free,
the possum ambled off, away.
The one I saw this morning lay
abandoned, waiting for the crows.
From death comes life. That's how it goes.
The circle makes good sense to me,
for otherwise, how could life be.
But help me why, hard-hearted, blithe,
do we inflict such death on life?

Beyond Pleasantrees

September 4

I laid my hand upon a tree
to listen, to feel its energy.
It wasn't long ere I discerned
a bit of what the tree had learned.
Nor sun nor rain forever stay
and night goes down and up comes day.
The winter's cold brings dormancy
and summer's heat an ecstasy.
The winds may come and crack a limb
or gently waft. And per their whims
the squirrels will scamper, dodge and leap.
And crows will caw, or owls sleep.
Through all of this the trees endure,
patient sentinels, secure.
And steady, rooted, giving, wise.
With hand on trunk, I recognize
my elders in their sylvan guise.

Sparrows at Sundown

September 14

Oh, how I love a roosting tree
where sparrows settle in for rest.
Their evening chirping comforts me
although I'm not the one addressed.
They have their gossip and concerns.
I eavesdrop on a foreign tongue,
a language I might never learn.
But since I get to live among
these chatterbirds, both morn and night,
I try to understand their moods,
what pains them, why their song is bright,
their dreams, and how they raise their broods.
I wonder, do they think at all
of me when I pass by? It may
be they ignore me as too tall
to matter in a sparrow's day.
And still, when day goes o'er to gloam
and evening brings its cooling airs,
the sparrows gathering in their home
enchant me. They're most welcome there.

Barred Owl on Irving Road

September 25

The village slept, and I did, too.
Until I heard, *Who cooks for you?*
She called and called. I doubt 'twas me
she meant to rouse. I rose to see
where she was perched, but in the dark
I only could stand near and hark,
and ask a question back to her
what is your message, and who for?

It's a Lot to Take In

October 1

October first dawns crisp and clear,
with classic autumn chill.
A day of beauty that appears
between the rains, and fills
the world around with easy splendor.
And all of this can be,
you think, because God's feeling tender.
In awe, and gratefully,
you watch the sun-blessed leaves, the sky,
the waning morning moon.
You want the hours to slow, not fly
this day will fade too soon.
And yet you know you can't command
nor time, nor night, nor day.
Though joy and beauty be at hand,
still, all things pass away.

September, October

October 2

No feud today between the sky and earth,
some wind, though mild enough, and yet, no mirth.
A mixed-up day, when clouds torment the sun
now summer's left and autumn has begun.
The trees still leafy in their dress of green
though neighbors north of us report they've seen
the colors start to change, and soon a frost
will come a pretty touch, but at a cost
petunias and tomatoes will expire.
Then won't we want a blanket or a fire?
But wait, the sun peeks through let's not yet mourn
September's passing while the air is warm.
The months process, one fades, the next comes in
as summer's yang gives way to darker yin.
Duality would seem to draw fixed lines
and still we seek to hold at the same time
both months, both seasons thus our feelings mix,
like sun and clouds we ought to learn such tricks
between our heart and mind just peace, no feud,
and balance to help us soften every mood.

Morning Glory

October 4

It's autumn now. The year is turning cold.
There's nothing new in that, this tale's been told.
Yet as night fades, each morning has its glory.
Again, there's nothing new in this old story.
I wonder, though I don't wish to be coy
why should we rise each day, unless for joy.
Something calls us daily from our bed.
Money, perhaps, the urge to get ahead,
or drearier, the need to make ends meet
so we and ours don't end up on the street.
It could be even duller stiff routine,
a rut which rubs from life its brighter sheen.
Here, too, there's nothing new there is much cause
to claim this day's no better than what was.
But if that's so, why struggle. Why endeavor
to face a gloom which seems to stretch forever?
We might, instead, embrace and celebrate
what comes, or goes, and so participate
in every day, two-handed, tough and willing.
Recall the mourning dove though sad will sing.

Sunday Starlings

October 5

I saw six starlings fly up high
against the pale blue Sunday sky.
They found a branch, and there did cry,
a morning song, but wry.
At first they'd lined up on one perch,
like congregants in pews at church.
But then a few began to lurch
away, as if in search
of individuality
although they looked alike to me .
Perhaps the morning's homily
encouraged them to see
what privileged bird's-eye views reveal
we are connected. We may feel
our differences. But Life's Ideal
includes us all within its wheel.

What a Day

October 7

October sun beats down, we feel alive
the insects, too, for now at least. They thrive.
They buzz and flit and fill the garden sky.
June-like, the world is bright and vivified.
Too bad the sleeping bats will miss this chance
to swoop and dart, and join the feasting dance.
But swifts and swallows, and the occasional jay
will eat their fill, they'll gobble up the day
an Indian summer day, a warm reprieve
that seems to stall the march of time, and leave
us full, like ripening fruit, and at our best
sweeter, grateful, ready for winter's test.

Listen—Bells!

Fling out your arms! Caper, dance and leap!
Twirl and shout and celebrate, and weep
at so much beauty. All by God ordained.
God and Nature, hand in hand, contained
in every creature, cloud and rock and vine
everywhere you look, the Spark Divine.
That same spark is in us. Join hands and sing
Creation's song. And dance in bliss. Yes, fling
your arms up, grab the waiting rope and cling
to it until the bells with praises ring.

October Surprise

October 7

After picking apples, then some spinach,
I found a bar, a terrace and a Guinness.
An Indian Summer sort of afternoon,
where garden wasps are active and festoon
the fruits and any thing that's sweet,
and sun and air and sky play at deceit.
I know it won't last long, this artful phase,
but while it lasts, I'll bask beneath the blaze
that otherwise must soon enough retire,
till in late Spring again we'll feel its fire.
Today, though, I won't weigh, compare, or measure
I'll sit content, in plenitude and pleasure.

Morning Melancholy

October 13

The trees lament the unkind wind,
the morning clouds rush north.
The eager dawn is damped and dimmed
she struggles to bring forth
both light and color for the day.
The moody sky beshrouds
her efforts, hiding blue away
behind the darkening clouds.
And we who struggled through the night
asleep, awake, afraid
and hoped for helpful morning light
have seen our dreams betrayed.

Reading the Locust Leaves

Little locust leaves sift down
littering driveway, deck and ground,
creating a tannish-yellow cast
green leaves above cannot now last.
Summer recedes to rosy past,
the gap to Winter shrinks. Too fast
the Autumn slips from gay to glum,
too fast the chilling gray will come.
Oh, Locusts Keep your leaves a while
so we may savor Autumn's smile.
Resist, for us, if not your sake,
the melancholy drift, and make
October's glow and glory bide
hold tight your leaves. Do not yet stand aside.

And the Winner Is . . .

October 14

It rained, a pounding rain the whole night through.
And now *The Morning Sun* shouts headline news
The Finest Month, October claims to be!
Top month for color, pomp and pageantry.
Exclusive interviews reveal Its fame
comes from the forest foliage all-aflame
in orange, yellow, russet, red and gold
a palette dipped and daubed a hundredfold
across the landscape. Extra! See! Behold
October's glory! Hear the story told
in its own words, and see the fashion show
of maple, aspen all the trees you know
of sycamore and birch and beech and oak!
See Autumn's finery, its dress and cloak!
Read all about it! See for your own eyes
October's triumph under sun-bleached skies!

(almost) Alone on Hadley Mountain

October 19

Are you like me? I like to go
when fewer folks are there.
It isn't selfishness I know
the woods are to be shared.
The summit views are there for all,
the lakes and rivers, too,
and autumn's leafy colored shawl.
But then it's also true
that time in nature on my own
helps me philosophize
that's why I often hike alone
though maybe that's unwise .
So, my feet climbed Hadley Mountain and
my heart climbed to the sky.
Again I felt my soul expand,
again, a nature high.

A Grim Foretelling

October 27

It may be time to sweep and rake
the locusts have dropped leaves.
The maples, orange, soon will shake
their arms, and Fall will heave
a heavy, leafy, shifting sigh.
And helpless, I will grieve.
The scudding clouds will dark the sky.
The only soft reprieve
will come when candlelight dispels
the gathering autumn gloom
that comes as wild November swells
and Winter nearer looms
when drear the mood and mute the bells
when grave the year-end doom
both sad and bitterly foretells
the death of light and bloom.

So Sorry, Miss B.

November 5

Three nights of frost how shall Miss B. survive?
Last fall we brought her in oh, how she thrived!
No day went by without her blossoming
begonias in the winter! Reckoning
from when she first called home our garden pot
she bloomed a year, five months, some days *a lot*
for gentle, tender-stemmed, pink-flowered B.
so lovely, loyal, such good company.
And now we've let her down, left her outside
through cold, cold nights. It may be that she cried
for us to fetch her in we didn't hear,
and now dejected, limp, her end is near.
At this point we can only make amends
by doing better by our other friends . . .

Oak on Vley Road

The oak on Vley is stately, tall and broad.
It bears a russet robe no maple gaud
of garish red, flame orange or bright gold
and keeps away, by rustling leaves, the cold
which now it seems, despite the sun today
has in the village booked a long-term stay.
But this oak firmly stands. A colder spell,
one winter more, can, truth to tell,
be shrugged off glibly, a little like late snow
which falls in March and irritates, then goes.
This oak has not much sylvan company
it overlooks its lot commandingly.
It nobly nods, and seems to acquiesce
to Nature's vagaries, with calm largesse.
One day its trunk will sway, its roots decay,
disease and storms may leach its strength away.
Look not today for that untimely death
admire, rather, its vigorous, sovereign breath,
its oaken power, reassuring might.
Emulate it, let the oak ignite
in you a spark, a light,
and lit up, stretch to reach your own best height.

Plotterkill Ode

November 11

The Plotterkill, Schenectady County's gem.
The ridge trails, north and south, combine to hem
the steep ravine, the waterfalls, the kill
an old Dutch word for creek, they say . And hills
above give views that elevate.
The fairies no doubt come to recreate
and revel. Angels, when they're near, must glide
and sigh. And hikers such as I can bide
at overlooks along the northern rim
and gazing, think they ought to pen a hymn,
a paean to the Plotterkill Preserve.
But no words I know are fine enough to serve.

Out There

November 11

The Pharaoh Lake Loop hike with Paul
sunshine, water, woods, and all
the richness forest walking brings.
Out there I find I think of things
with other thoughts. With different eyes
I see. The motions synthesize
my movement through the world and life,
with my self-image. Tramping's rife
with time to ponder and assess
the trees, now stripped of autumn dress,
are bare, reposing and revealed,
and my hike under them may yield
an answer yet. I, too, am bare
or barer when I walk out there.
And when I've walked both far and long,
I'll hear, I hope, at long last, my own song.

Head First

November 13

Stripped of all defenses, clothes
I plunged. The frigid water rose
up to my neck. And I suppose
you'll ask, What for? It's this I chose
today and Pharaoh Lake to tick
November off my list. I picked
a warmer, sunny time to swim
this lake, and so work toward my whim
twelve months of Adirondack baths,
a challenge on a different path.
This one was Cold, and March and May
when I swam took my breath away.
They nearly froze me. Though the coldest
still await, which means my boldest
dips December scary
January, February
may mean a health and safety risk.
And I know folks will warn and tsk
and shake their heads It's foolish, folly.
Perhaps the cold can kill. But golly!
Going in, you're so alive
and getting out, you have survived!
Adrenalin and vigor course
and pierce you with you is the Force.
The mountain water's cold empowers,
you blossom like a winter flower.
Nan Shepherd's term Annihilation
of one's self. Mine? Inspiration.

Snow Falling on Cedar Ridge

November 16

A lake, a gentle snowfall through the night.
A morning, gray, yet also winter-white.
A deck, a view of water, still, serene,
a mirror, where the trees and hills are seen.
A cedar, dipped in snow, now deeper green.
A heart, filled up, and beating in between
an earthly heaven, soft in early light
a heavenly earth, a sweet celestial sight.

November, Again

November 17

Ivy green and maple yellow
in mid-November cheer a fellow.
No disrespect to Spring's full palette
but these strong colors, like a mallet,
strike you you recall October
before the cold and storms disrobed her
most trees now stand there, bare, austere.
Yet bright and shiny leaves lie here
maple gold on ivy green
if this is something you have seen,
then join me in my admiration.
Leave aside your consternation
at cloudy days and colder nights
November does have its delights.
Among the months it is downtrodden
skies of gloom and pathways sodden,
melancholy, murk and mist
at times you want to shake your fist.
Yet month eleven casts a spell,
mixing lurid with pastel.

National Take-a-Hike Day

November 17

Honestly, I see more wildlife in my yard.
And we have locusts, maples and a mulberry.
As well as flower beds and ferns, and vines of squash.
The seats are also there, to sit and take it in when there is time.
And still I hear the call to hike.
Is it the thousand thousand thousand trees,
the wood itself, that calls, inviting me
to mingle in its near eternal, subtle sylvan murmuring?
Or maybe crows or ravens, salamanders, peepers, bugs,
all asking for my quiet company?
The chorus of the brook and lake,
the singing of the mountains fair?
Perhaps it is the trail itself that wants to
know again the dedicated tread of boots and beat of heart.
In any case, the line is open and the call
comes loud, comes clear,
comes quickening the claim that Nature makes.
And why should I resist? I go.
On other days, I have to be content with planning,
poring over maps and books of trails
of real, or just imaginary routes.
Those days I'm craving hoisting pack and donning boots.
So what to make of this official hiking day?
It's not a bad idea, I hear you say.
And I agree, I guess. But I would like to add
that any day is good to take a hike.

Full Moon Morning

November 20

Low above the cemetery,
bright and round, she isn't scary.
Benevolent, she shines for all,
a full moon worthy of this fall.
In just an hour she'll slip away.
Right now, though, I can hear her say
I know that there's a bond between us
last night as I shone down with Venus,
I looked and saw you that you were gazing
up. I heard you greet me, praising
me for beauty that I borrow.
And now again, this early morrow,
there you are, with admiration.
You bring me, I said, inspiration.
You overrate me, she replied.
I have no brilliance deep inside
I'm superficial, mere reflection.
Yet I esteem the introspection
I get from you, our close connection.
You're deep enough, I said. Perfection
isn't what I'm looking for.
She sighed. *The burden of the lore*
that has grown up weighs heavily.
I do my best, but you can see
I stopped her. Heaven has ordained
that you shine back what's to be gained
by second guessing? Be content
with what you are. *If your intent,*
she answered, nodding, *is to cheer me,*

thank you. I said, Listen, hear me
I'm oh so grateful that you shine
on our dark world with beams benign.

The Bones of November

November 28

My brother's here, to see November's bones
the leafless trees. To hear the aching moans
of darkening wind. To step on icy stones.
To breathe in frost, and with it sharp laments.
To feel the melancholy pierce each sense.
To hail the harsh transition of the year.
To revel in November raw, austere.
Inevitably taking up its place,
constricting life with chill, and clearing space
for winter, and the cycle's end. To face
the change within. To recognize and own
our imperfections. To hope that we have grown.
To pray that in the end we're not alone.

Snowy Yard

Some folks will take it grumpy hard
to wake and see their once green yard
is mostly white from fresh clean snow.
It means that winter's near, they know.
The very thought they find alarming.
They resist it. Yet it's charming!
Snow on roofs is picturesque,
trees become more statuesque,
garden beds are dressed up, brighter.
The street seems formal, sharper, lighter.
At times the world looks harsh and scarred
a paradise that we have marred.
But snow can blanket all, like kersey,
mantling blemishes with mercy.
Paradoxically then, snow,
warms me, head to heart to toe.

Old Friends

December 2

I saw the Moon, just past half full.
Her mighty enigmatic pull
the ocean feels it, and the tides,
and I, the way she silver-glides
across the sky on year-end nights,
outshining neighbors' Christmas lights,
and beaming down, bright-faced and steady.
She waits for me. And when I'm ready,
I bundle up, go out and walk.
She smiles down. That's when we talk.
With age comes wisdom her advice
illuminates. Let it suffice
I don't know anyone like her,
or many folk I would prefer
to walk with winter nights and morns.
I trust her she's not like the norns,
who plotted Norsemen's destiny.
She seems to like to share with me.
I helped her once now some years since ,
back when she lacked the confidence
to be herself. Our friendship's sound.
I treasure it. She is profound
yet sailing high, she's down-to-earth.
We recognize each other's worth.
We speak, but we can also be
content in silent company.
True friends are we, the Moon and I,
one here below, one in the sky.

Red Squirrel, What Next?

December 4

I've heard you scrabble, seen you scamper
here in my garage. Your nest
is in the loft. Your place of rest
and messy, nut-strewn rodent hamper.
I've warned you, You can't stay.
That paper-grass-and-nut collection
meant, I know, for your protection
in winter has been cleared away.
At this late date it may seem cruel
to force you to evacuate
your lofty, cosy, choice estate.
But I have opted for renewal
of order and my sovereignty.
And you, so agile, sharp and clever
surely you will relocate.
Though perhaps you'll curse that fate
which coaxed you to endeavor
to lodge in close proximity
to one unwelcoming as me.

Deer Brother

December 7

Oh, Little Brother, take my thanks.
I know you had no time to wonder
Must it be me? And *Why?* Your flanks
were pierced before you heard the thunder.
You dropped, and instantly were dead.
I knelt to hold your noble head.
I softly spoke, and stroked your neck
perhaps your spirit saw and heard,
and felt my strange remorse. But flecked
with blood, your body never stirred.
It isn't much, but here's my gratitude
for your great gift. Through death is life renewed.

Little Sister

December 13

The owl called, the turkey, then the crow.
In morning fog I sat along the slow
and somber, cold December creek
and watched for you. A game of hide-and-seek.
You won, hands down. You never came in sight.
My scope and rifle waited for the right
chance meeting. Smartly, you stayed put. Next year,
if plans I have go well, we'll both be here.
We'll test each other once again. Will we
survive, the pair of us, till then? We'll see.
For now I wish you life, a mate, a fawn.
And when day breaks, the joy in every dawn.

Yule

December 21

Icicles hanging from the roof
and solstice chill are pointed proof
that Winter's come. And still I sit
and watch scrap wood in the fire pit
go up in gorgeous flame, and melt
the snow nearby. A Druid Celt
would surely mark the season's turn
with greater ritual. To burn
some fence bits, drink an ale,
and see the crescent moon in pale
and noble tolerance look down
on us the Druids would be bound
to miss the dance, the standing stones,
the chants and sacrifice. Alone
I welcome Winter and the light.
And ponder much on solstice night.

What We Can't Do Without

Though cold, there's open water on the creek,
and on the lake. And so I went to seek
the herons, great ones. I know that they live there.
They heard me crunching snow. As they got scared,
they took to flight. First one, then two. They flew
away from me. That's normal, nothing new.
I came last year to them, to see their grace.
And yes, I know I should avoid their space
and let them live their heron lives in peace.
But seeing them's a gift they help increase
my calm, somehow. I won't come every day,
just now and then, at most. And I won't stay.
It does me good to have them live nearby
roosting, grawking, regal when they fly,
feeding in the shallows, finding fish
enough at least for heron happiness.
As herons, they're complete. They don't need me.
I'm human I need them, quite obviously.

Blanket of Mercy

It's true enough that New Year's Day was Friday,
and that's the day when new beginnings start.
But school resumes today, the Congress, too.
And probably a lot of folks have barely
written down their resolutions list,
let alone commenced to change their lives.
The snow that came and fell here yesterday
brought us this Monday morning fairy tale,
a scene of beauty. Boughs and branches bent,
a glistening from porch lights and a cosy,
muffling of the waking world. How snow,
which costs us time and strength to clear away,
can also soften everything it lands on
is a little miracle, I think.
It may not last, it never lasts, in fact.
But every time it gently falls, it blankets
us and our small patch of world which we
tend to believe is all the world with mercy
as if forgiving absolution wafts
with every crystal flake. This is
a very good and humbling way to start,
with hope, the first week of the new-born year.

Supper, Then a Windy Walk

January 8

The moon was almost full post-dinner, so was I
and contra-danced with clouds, away up high.
The wind kicked up and called me, so I went.
The chilling air, the moon-lit snow were meant,
I think, to show the winter night
which wasn't dark at all in its best light.
The moon illuminated woods and glades.
And I laughed to see it bright enough for shade.
In no time I was down behind the lake
to catch the wind skate o'er the ice and shake
my cap, so that I'd grab it tight.
I reveled in its frosty whip and bite.
When moon and wind conspire to invite
well, who'd resist such wintery delights?

The Moon and I

January 9

Two nights now I have walked beneath the moon.
High up she drifts like Heaven's white balloon.
I'd hold her hand if she were not so high
but being her, I'd also keep the sky
as my domain and leave the earth below
to its own joys and trials, letting go
and riding light of heart and free of care.
Yet walking where I am I still may dare
to follow her example. I'll be bright.
I'll beam and smile on all. Like a kite
I'll dance, uplifting spirits as I rise.
Wait, though. It comes as no surprise
that when winds shift, a kite will falter. All
of us must stumble now and then, and fall.
Sometimes the moon must struggle with the clouds
to be her radiant self. And life can shroud
us, too. Not every day is grand.
Things often happen not as we have planned.
Nevertheless, the moon sticks to her task.
And can we, too? Is that too much to ask?

Fire-Pit

Our early January cold is cold.
Though not the frigid cold
that folk endured in Neolithic times,
when fur and fire in cave or hut
were all that kept their blood
from giving in to Winter's icy grasp.
Yet still ours bites. It chills, it hurts, it kills.
Why then, you ask, do I decide
to sit outside today beneath a bright
but fading sky that brings no warmth.
Vermilion stripes of cirrus tint the west.
As night draws in, I see each breath
they tell me I'm alive.
And even with cold toes and colder back
I revel in the grandeur of the air.
The afternoon that bows to dusk and dark
is like to me I recognize the force
that's great enough to set these things in gear,
and bow in thankfulness, and breathe.
My life is full of comforts.
Meaning it is good, I find, to tend a fire
that cannot keep the cold at bay.
To know again the power of Life and all that moves in it.
And feel the cold on cheeks and ears,
the truth of my great insignificance.
The Universe is in my head, of course,
but when I sit outside
and make a winter fire in deepest cold,
It shows its very face to me.

Saunter

January 26

Amble, stroll and stride and walk.
Range, and run and lope.
Wander, ramble, climb and hike.
Plod and trudge and step.
And saunter there's a word that's grand.
It's from the French, some say
sans terre I'm "without home or land."
Or else *a la sainte terre*
"the Holy Lands we're off to them."
Or what about *santren*
"to muse, to be in reverie."
The experts can't agree.
I'll tell you, though, I like this term,
no matter where it's from.
To saunter through the fields and woods,
on hills and through a village,
to drink the draught of deeper thoughts
on aimless pilgrimage . . .
From satisfying hours and miles
I'm flushed, enthused, restored.
I touch the jeweled world and smile.
I think I'll saunter more.

Plotterkill Magic

January 27

A hundred steps, on snow, in woods,
I feel it. I think, Frodo could
perceive this magic, Sam likewise.
Listen you can hear his cries
"Adventure, Mr. Frodo, elves!
Today they might just show themselves,
you never know." See Frodo smiles,
and nods. The wending way beguiles
and I expect that Sam is right.
The woodland elves and fairy sprites
don't leave their prints, but they are near
and if I'm still they may appear.
If not, no matter. I can wait
for other days. I trust my fate,
like Frodo's, will conspire to bring
the joy of me encountering
them in a glistening winter glade
or in high summer, in the shade
of fir or oak. What speech between
us there will be, of air pristine
and woodsy bliss and skies above,
and all in nature that we love.

Wind

February 9

The wind insists the sky be swept
and so it blows to east from west
unceasingly. It wants no rest.
And if one little cloud were kept
to show its bit of white on blue
reflecting sun, greeting the new
day with a puff, oh Wind, would you
feel challenged in your mightiness?
Be easy, I wouldn't think the less
of you. I've seen your snapping whip
the trees then tremble, dance and skip,
loose leaves will fly and odd debris
and even shingles are set free.
Your chilling blasts enliven me.
You have a power we should fear
yet when I walk and you are there
you fill my lungs with charged-up air
relentless, fierce. I'm glad you're near.

Ready?

A sleetstorm has made morning walking dicey
on speckled sidewalks, crunchy, slick and icy.
A lesson overnight, conditions alter,
and our routine must, too. If not, we falter,
at a loss, unsure how to proceed.
Listen, Life is saying, *You still need*
another lens to see, a letting-go,
a willingness to dance with me, and grow.
Your morning needn't be the same each day
in fact, with time and trust, you'll maybe say,
I'm ready, I'll embrace what comes my way.
Recall, "Thy will be done" is what you pray.

Map and Compass

Tyler knows his stuff and teaches well
enthused, engaged, informed and down-to-earth.
His humor bubbles up, he shines with light.
And so we learned and laughed and got our bearings,
out in the field and also on the map.
And now, with practice, maybe,
setting off for bushwhacking adventures
we can find the way
not only there, but back again.
Two sixty-plus year-olds
we could just follow well-known, marked
and clearly trodden trails.
What is the point, at this late point,
in training to step off the safest path?
But risk is where the new beginnings lie.
And new beginnings bring a new horizon.
To take a bearing in the field you look
Ahead.
You want to reach another place.
You set your course and leapfrog obstacles.
Imagination, innovation call
new possibility and new direction.
And thus a course in map and compass skills
will serve for several kinds of journeys
those on foot, out in the sun and rain,
and subtler crossings of interior terrain.

Canopies of Green

February 20

The trees already know, of course,
but when I walk I say to them,
Your winter sleep is coming to an end.
The growing daylight's their alarm,
the only one they need, unless
you count some days of running sap
before the equinox arrives.
I bet that nudges them awake
I picture them in stretching mode,
their branches reaching out or up,
the way I do my yoga tree.
You'd think their friendship with the wind
would keep away the twiggy kinks.
Through winter days their sturdy trunks
stood firm while gales convinced their limbs
to sway and dance. I was enchanted
by their intricate design
of spreading, arching, intertwining arms.
But be that as it may, these friends
again will soon pass through the rite of spring.
Their leafing out will green my yard
in fact, the world and soften view and life.
Right now, this bare-limbed, bright and blue-skied
February morning is enough.
But knowing, looking forward, who
can't help but quicken at the thought
of canopies of green to come.

Rabbit Tracks

February 20

Where he lives I do not know
but he leaves tracks on each new snow.
I see them when I go outside
so somewhere near he must reside.
His prickings show he comes and goes
and if I tracked them, I suppose
they'd lead me to his winter den.
But if I found his home, why then,
alas, my wondering would end.
Not knowing's better. I pretend
the tracks are in a wilder wood
where other wild creatures could
meander through to leave their prints
I'd love to see a wolf but since
there are none here, let Rabbit be
the link between the wild and me.

Arabella

February 21

You look, black-eyed.
I am bemused to find you here,
not knowing even that you had arrived.
I stand and question you.
You measure me, then turn away.
A month till spring.
And were you homeless till you found
our little spot out of the cold?
The red squirrel hasn't been about for weeks.
Perhaps you chased him off,
as I should chase you off as well.
Your bandit face and perky ears
and ring-striped tail all come with teeth.
And surely our garage is not the place for this.
Unless. How long
before you birth your kits?
I'll grant you time for that
six weeks or so.
But then our ways must part.
Your silence nods.
It's what you've always had in mind.

Three Generations, Out Walking the Land

February 22

We walked, the four of us, on family land,
Straight out, then through the red-pine woods,
across what once were fields, and to a pond.
Along the way we saw the waterfalls of ice
although the day was warm
and skiers coming off the lifts.
And lots of tracks, coyote, mostly,
deer, of course, some other creatures' signs.
We reached the iced-up pond, and both girls danced.
My niece, who owns it all,
was rediscovering it, it had been years.
And for the younger grand-niece, this was new
the older one has walked with me before.
The trail I made years back is faded,
only paws would know it now.
And plants in these parts grow,
so brush and bush and undergrowth are thick
in spots. But with a will we made it through,
collecting twigs in hair and burrs on fleece,
and memories, I hope. With any luck
we four will walk the land again.
And time, which ebbs and flows and forces us
to strike new trails and leave old ones behind,
is kind in that regard, I do believe.
A challenge lifts our life, and at day's end,
when all is said and done, in gratitude
we nod. It was a lovely walk.

I Know, I Know

March 3

Don't hike alone in winter. Good advice.
Which I discounted yesterday. Again.
I grabbed the poles and snowshoes, hit the trail
an easy out-and-back to Dexter Lake.
An hour or so in winter solitude
belied by tracks of snowmobiles on trails and lakes.
But this mid-day, mid-week, it was just me.
A frost-tinged, fairy forest fir and beech
and silence when I stopped and stood and sighed.
And at trail's end, there was no end
the snowmobilers carried on. The sign said point eight miles.
That, I said aloud, will help me reach
the backside of old Spectacle and loop the lake.
No longer out-and-back I'll go around.
Until I found the riders had no plan
to link the trails that I would need.
Instead they brought me through a frozen marsh
and thence out on the lake itself.
I thought it over, once, then twice.
But if the ice held them, then why not me.
The open views were stark, and bleak
I liked them, and the wind blew well,
and looking back I loved the line
my tracks had made across the snow's expanse.
And bit by bit my mind attuned to landscape more than ice.
At times I clicked the poles through snow
to check the icy strength, but more and more
I scanned the shoreline, and admired islands
trapped in winter's too-tight hug.

Or skeletons of trees whose dormant days were long behind.
And then, of course, it happened Crack.
The ice gave way, my shoes went in
and instantly I threw myself ahead, and flat
they always say that prone you have a chance.
My snowshoes benefited from the chunks of ice,
a little buoyancy that kept them from a dive.
I hauled them out, got to my feet
and saw I'd strayed too close to shore.
My breath was deep, I don't know what I said.
The water wasn't deep, but could have been.
And still I had a good half mile of lake to go.
The boots are waterproof,
and they and gaiters kept me mostly dry.
Which I must say is good, since no one
wants a three-mile hypothermic walk.
I paid a little more attention after that,
until I left the lake and caught the trail.
And all was well.
By half past two I made it to the car,
alive with pleasure from my outdoor day.
I even had an ice cream, just to celebrate.
Though eating it, I thought,
You shouldn't, really, hike alone in winter.

"True Listening Is Worship"*

March 15, 2022

Listen with your soul, it knows your needs.
Watch the creatures, see the life it leads.
Already they inhabit, as John writes,
the eternal. Unself-conscious, they are free.
The music of the universe invites
come into rhythm, into unity.

Touch the trees, and they'll touch you in turn.
Feel the breeze, and add your breath to it.
Hear frogs serenade, and sing with them.
Mosquitoes have their place, so be at peace.
Taste the nectar of the dawn and gulp it down.
See in every face life's symphony.
Smell the memories, join your timeless self.
Find the doorstep, balance there between
the inner and the outer infinite.
Know that you yourself can link those two.
Live a pace that gives you time to be
learn that doing can create a veil.
Listen to your body, wrapped in soul.
Listen with your soul, and become whole.

from *Anam Cara* by John O'Donohue

Joseph Carosella had a long and enjoyable career teaching German, English, and the occasional life lesson to young people. Now he reads, hikes, travels, gardens, and orders the largest ice cream cones possible. He also writes a lot, talks even more, and contemplates pretty much everything. He and his wife live in Scotia, New York.

Shanti Arts

Nature · Art · Spirit

Please visit us online
to browse our entire book catalog,
including poetry collections and fiction,
books on travel, nature, healing, art,
photography, and more.

Also take a look at our highly regarded art
and literary journal, *Still Point Arts Quarterly*,
which may be downloaded for free.

www.shantiarts.com